The Heart
of the Matter

Thoughts To Live By

Bill O'Hearn

Entheos Publishing Company

Entheos Publishing Company
32251 S.W. Boones Bend Road
Wilsonville, Oregon 97070

Dedication

To Elizabeth,
my beautiful wife,
partner and friend.
Thank you
for all you are
and for all
you have helped me become.
I love you.

~

And to
my Step-dad, Eveard Fish,
for his gentle ways,
his great mind
and his being an important part
of my life for the past
fifty-five years.

ACKNOWLEDGEMENTS

There are so many of my long-time friends who are so important to what this book is all about. Our years together have helped shape who I am, and how I think today. When I look back over the past forty-plus years that many of us have been together, I can do nothing but count my blessings. I wish I could acknowledge all of you here in print, but I guess that is not feasible. Anyway, thank you one and all. You know who you are and how important you are to me and how much I love you.

I do want to mention my children, Molly, Patti, Julie and Chip, and thank them for what they taught me while I thought I was teaching them — and for then adding more teachers to the family in the form of sons-in-law, a daughter-in-law and six grandchildren. My learning keeps on.

Now to others who had input in one form or another.

First of all to my wife, Elizabeth, whose thoughts, always offered graciously, nudged me this way and that. Did I always listen? Mostly. Did I always appreciate? Always.

Then there is my editor, Thorn Bacon, The Master of the Red Pen. How we could stay friends while he continually cut out my heart with his Zoro-like slashes, I don't know. But we did and I survived. Thank you, Thorn. Because of you I have grown — although you may have successfully stopped me from attempting to write a book titled *How To Keep High Self-Esteem In The Face Of Constant Rejection.*

And to Ursula Bacon, a very special human being, thank you for your friendship and for your wonderful imagination in bringing this book's cover from an idea to its final beauty through Richard Ferguson's artistic touch.

And thank you, Richard, for the third time, for changing thought into reality. You too are special.

Extra thanks to Sheryl Mehary for formatting this book and always having a smile and a hug for me.

Cliff Canucci. You win again. Thank you for suggesting just the right title for this book, as you did for *From The Heart Of A Lion* — and for your enthusiasm for the content and valuable input while this book was still a manuscript.

Greg Hansen. Always encouraging. Always thoughtful. Always there. And now ready to burst through to new heights in his own evolvement.

To Kathy Hove, who received great pleasure, once again, in pointing out the error of my grammatical ways. (I didn't always listen.)

To Robert G. (as in Gordon, as in Flash) Hicks, of Charbonneau, who constantly wanted to know if his name would appear in my next book. Plus, he's a nice guy.

To Gary and Shelley Bold, for their thoughts, their support and their friendship.

To Lee Ross, a soon-to-be-well-known artist, for her encouraging ways and beautiful spirit. Arizona has gained a blessing.

To Jody Miller Stevenson, author of a great new book, *Soul Purpose,* for insisting that I already knew my purpose and pushing me to follow it.

To Lani Jean O'Callaghan, for her courage and example in following her own light.

And finally to Lyle Nelson, whose wonderful spirit has touched me and so many others. Thank you for your example of what *The Heart Of The Matter* is really all about.

TABLE OF CONTENTS

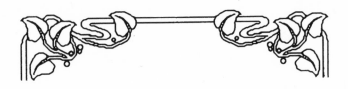

The cover of this book is all about
potential.
A record-breaking sunflower was
grown in 1982 which measured 27-
1/2 inches in diameter and contained
over 10 million seeds.
The sunflower represents the possibilities which reside in each of us.
The butterfly is a reminder that trans-
formation from what we appear to be
to what we can be is what the
journey is all about.
This book was written to help you on
that journey.

PREFACE

I have been concerned in much of my adult life with trying to be better, do better and learn more. My thought was that there was a destination to be reached. I now realize there is no end. In my first book, *From the Heart of a Child,* I said that the "farther I go the farther I can see." I appreciate even more now that there will always be new perspectives, new discoveries. The seeking is the blessing.

The insights I share with you in this book are a continuation of the map of where I am. They are how I *feel* at this stage of my life, knowing that circumstances and people and my own thoughts will shape my future perspective.

My need to share my thoughts with you is probably based on a compulsion to teach, but at the core of that compulsion is a deep desire to

~ ~

help you make your way easier. That will happen if I can convince you to believe in all that you are and to become all that you can become.

Life is a treasure hunt. My mission is to help you realize that the treasure to be uncovered lies where you might least seek it — right within your own heart. Your *Spirit* is the priceless gem and *You* are what your journey is all about.

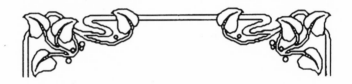

There is so much more
to what this is all about
than what this is all about.

— *Bill O'Hearn*

CHAPTER 1

The longer I live the more I suspect that I just don't know what life is all about. Do you sometimes feel the same way?

I am beginning to realize, however, that somehow there is more to what this is all about, than what we *think* this is all about. I'm not referring to an enhanced relationship with our Creator, because I think that is the most important part of what this is all about anyway. But I sense that our existence here is to be different, or more — somehow.

The farther I travel my own path, and the more I experience life, the more convinced I am that we are just at the beginning of what is possible. I believe that the future of what this is all about will be centered on people rather than things. We will learn how to use our thoughts to

~ ~

shape our world and grow personally in ways which are beyond our ability at this point to imagine. And eventually we will learn to love each other, and serve each other. Isn't that a nice thought? I'm learning to believe this is really possible. And if I believe and you believe and others too, then what this is all about will someday be *what this is really all about.*

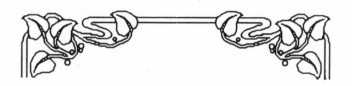

He who has so little knowledge
of human nature
as to seek happiness
by changing anything
except his own disposition
will waste his life
in fruitless efforts,
and multiply the grief
he proposes to remove.

— *Samuel Johnson*

CHAPTER 2

Look around you at the unhappiness of many of the people you are acquainted with. If you were to observe some of these people closely you would discover that many times it is the little things, unimportant things, which become major stumbling blocks in their lives.

Can you imagine a tube of toothpaste causing someone to contemplate divorce? Well, it did and I did within the first year of my marriage to Gloria. Gloria is gone now, but in our courting stage everything was perfect, and I was on my best behavior trying to prove that I was the man for her. That changed once we had been married for a short time. For some reason I went from trying to please her to pleasing me. From giving to taking. I wanted *her* to be perfect, and she wasn't. One trait of hers literally

~ ~

drove me to thoughts of divorce. I had learned to squeeze the toothpaste tube neatly from the bottom. Gloria grew up squeezing it haphazardly. This gave me the opportunity at least twice a day to get really upset. It took me a long, long time to understand that where a toothpaste tube is squeezed is not grounds for ruining a relationship.

You may laugh at my silliness, but before you do, look at your important relationships and ask yourself if you are placing unreasonable expectations on others. If you are, you'd better change your thinking. Because if your happiness depends upon someone else changing, you are in for some unhappy times.

Unless, of course, you learn to squeeze the toothpaste tube any old place — as I have.

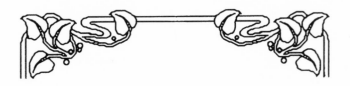

Sometimes

Across the fields of yesterday
He sometimes comes to me
A little lad just back from play,
The lad I used to be.
And yet he smiles so wistfully
Once he's crept within.
I wonder if he hoped to see
The man I might have been.

– Thomas Samuel Jones (circa 1899)

Chapter 3

I decided a long time ago that the words which appear on the left page would not be my personal anthem. Yet, I keep thinking there is more to me than I've shown the world so far. Sometimes this is an encouraging thought — there is excitement and accomplishment waiting in the wings. Sometimes, too often, it is a discouraging thought. Time is flying by and I'm not living up to my full potential.

When I do measure myself against the dreams of the lad I used to be, I am drawn to think of that unbelievably creative Leonardo da Vinci, who was reported to have said on his death bed that he couldn't die yet because he had so much more to do. Even the great don't get it all done. Yet I don't want to use that as a rationalization. The potential is waiting.

~ ~

How about you? How do you feel about your progress so far? If you're young and just getting started you probably feel pretty good. You've got the whole world before you. But if you've had a few years on the firing line, you may feel a bit wistful about the way things are going.

My thought for you is that it is important for you to stay aware that there is far more to you than you've shown the world, and you must stay alert to possibilities which will help you grow. Life becomes more and more interesting — and more and more fulfilling — when you continually strive to become the best that you can become.

Rather than a wistful smile from that little lad or lass that was, wouldn't it feel great to get a "high five"?

~ ~

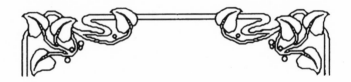

Nothing is impossible to the person
who will not listen to reason.

– *Hawkeye of M*A*S*H*

CHAPTER 4

I don't remember where I heard that the United States Congress, in the early 1900s, came within one vote of doing away with the Patent Office. The thought was that everything had been invented and the Patent Office was unnecessary. In today's age of high technology it is difficult to imagine that sort of shortsightedness. Yet, we are all guilty of practicing that very same kind of limited thinking every day in our personal lives. We forget that there is genius disguised as imagination within each of us.

Let me ask you a question. Can you name a major influence in your life who, at one time or another, insisted that you listen to reason and logic, convincing you that an exciting idea wouldn't work? Was it a parent or friend? A spouse, brother or sister? Anyone you care about

~ ~

and sometimes people you don't care about, can kill an idea with logic and reason — *if you let them!*

Let me urge you to be wary of "Reason." It can keep you from taking the next step on your path. When Reason says, "Impossible," just smile to yourself and say, "I know better!"

Remember, you can't argue with Reason. Reason has its feet on the ground. It *knows.* But Imagination has wings. It can *fly.*

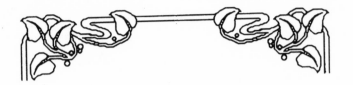

Things which matter most
must never be
at the mercy
of things which matter least.
Goethe

CHAPTER 5

I've heard it said that the average adult couple spends fewer than 15 minutes a week in any kind of meaningful dialogue. Something that matters most is placed at the mercy of things that surely matter less — bigger homes, better cars, advancement in the corporate world. Often we spend more time over lunch with a stranger than we do with our spouse or children. It seems that our whole existence is dedicated to pursuit of the least at the expense of the most.

If life seems like a race to get more and you're enjoying it less, and you are interested in becoming all that you can be — you are going to have to make some pretty important decisions.

Commencing change is always difficult, but I've found a good way to begin is with a personal inventory. I like to use the Benjamin

~ ~

Franklin T-square method. It can be a five minute exercise with long-lasting effects.

Take a blank sheet of paper and draw a line down the middle. Then draw a line across the top to form a "T." Title the left column "Most" and the right column "Least." What I am going to ask you to do is to examine your values and determine which are most important to you, and then list them in the left column. You might list things like Good Health, or Loving Relationships or whatever. Just make sure that they are values you want for yourself.

List the least important things in your life in the right column. You may discover that there are things in this column which you really enjoy but are really not "matter most" items. One that comes to my mind is television. It is a major player in the lives of many people. Do you think it is possible for TV to keep someone from becoming all that she can become?

An acquaintance of mine, the nationally known speaker Lou Heckler, demonstrates how such a list as you might make can be condensed even more. Lou has the people in his audience fold a sheet of paper into four squares, then tear the paper so that there are four individual sheets. Then he asks the audience to list the four most important things in their lives — one on each page. Most people will list things like Health, a

~ ~

strong relationship with God, etc. Then he asks the audience to look at each sheet and throw away the least important. At this point there are a lot of "Oh no's."

Then he asks people to look at the remaining three and do the same thing — crumple up and throw away the least important piece of paper. Now it is down to two, and the audience is getting restless. Which one will they throw away and which one will they keep? When everyone is down to one remaining sheet, Lou asks this question, "How much time, each day, are you spending with your most important value?"

You can hear a lot of groans. When I was seated in the audience, listening to Lou, I looked at my remaining value. It made me wonder what in the world I was doing with my life on a daily basis. One thing was obvious — I sure wasn't spending a lot of time pursuing my "top" value. You might try this exercise yourself. It could start you down a very interesting path.

So become aware of what matters most, and remember:

The good things in life are the mortal enemy of the great things in life.

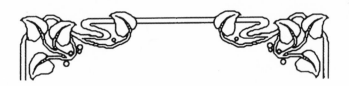

You will not be punished
for your anger,
you will be punished
by your anger.

— *Buddha*

CHAPTER 6

Anger, the destroyer of spirit and flesh. We are all familiar with stories of the unthinking parent whose fits of anger eventually undermine the fragile self-esteem of a child, or the boss whose concern for the bottom line ignores the human equation and in the process destroys the happiness of his employees. The victims of anger are everywhere you look.

But there is another victim of anger, and this person may end up suffering more than the target of anger. This is the one who vents the anger, who is preparing the scene for all sorts of personal and physical repercussions.

If you happen to be the angry one, regardless of the object of your anger, its poison reflects back on you. Your physical chemistry gets thrown out of balance. Your heartbeat

~ ~

increases. Your blood pressure rises. Your rational thinking process is thrown out of kilter. And — perhaps most importantly — your ability to resist disease may be reduced. I think this is what Buddha meant when he said, "You will be punished by your anger."

The side effects of anger are enormous, so it's in your best interest to:

> ***Discover a way to get rid of anger in***
> ***your life,***
> ***Or your anger may get rid of your life.***

Anger can cause not only estrangement from what could have been a loving relationship, but also from one's self. The person who gets mad a lot must have some thoughts now and then about not being the person he would like to be.

Three choices present themselves when you feel anger coming on:

1- You can get mad.

2- You can stifle your anger and hold it inside.

3- You can defuse your anger.

Most psychologists agree that it's better to go ahead and get mad rather than hold it inside. Better still, why not find a way to defuse anger?

The first step to accomplish this requires that you step outside yourself and ask yourself some important questions:

~ ~

What kind of a person do I really want to be?

Do I really want to hurt the object of my anger?

Do I really want to damage my health and possibly shorten my life?

Does anger serve the purpose for my existence?

Does anger serve my Ego or my Spirit?

The second step in ridding yourself of anger behavior is to practice turning it aside in your imagination. Try, in your mind, replaying an event which evoked anger, except this time picture yourself acting with patience and under-standing and then feeling good for having extended your potential as a human being.

If unwanted anger is a challenge in your life, don't consider your efforts a failure if you are unable to put the answers to the above questions to work immediately. It takes time to alter behavior even when you know you'll benefit by the change.

You have it within you to evolve from a judgmental person to an understanding one, from a blaming human to a forgiving spirit. But whatever happens when you tap this power, I bet you will find that you'll like your world, and you, a whole lot better.

∞

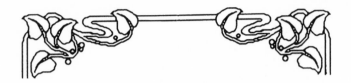

Where there is no vision,
the people perish.

– Proverbs 29:18

Chapter 7

Helen Keller was once asked if there was anything worse than being blind. She replied, "Yes, being able to see and having no vision."

I sometimes quote a little phrase whose origin is unknown to me: "Died at 25 — buried at 75." It's obvious that this epitaph refers to people who quit dreaming not long after they started their adult lives. It refers to people who have no vision of their possibilities and choose to exist rather than to really live.

Yet there are messages from all the great teachers telling us that living with vision is vital if we are to become all that we can become.

These messages, no matter what the source, simply state:

~ ~

You were born to accomplish.
You were born to dream.
You were born to live your vision —
To discover the specialness of you.
You were born to make a difference.

It is my belief that anything you dream you can do — you can do! I'm not talking about those dreams which happen while you're asleep. I'm talking about those dreams which happen when you are wide awake. Dreams that come to you when you allow your imagination to soar. Dreams that hint at something you'd *really* like to *do* or *be*. Maybe it is to paint, or to play beautiful music or start a child care center. Maybe it is an idea that will make a difference in the lives of thousands.

Within your reach is the power to create your vision. But first you must be willing to *listen* to your imagination and pay attention to your intuition. You must let go of the negative thoughts which belittle your power, and begin to ask, "What is possible?" Then you must learn to trust yourself *and* the wisdom of the Universe — to let your fearful Ego go, and let your courageous Spirit take over.

When that happens, you will begin to hear the music. And when you begin to hear the music you can begin to dance your dance. And

~ ~

when you begin to dance your dance — you will begin to experience the meaning of your existence.

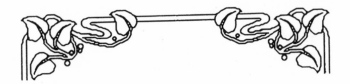

Sometimes we get
so caught up in results,
we fail to enjoy the process.
— *Bill O'Hearn*

CHAPTER 8

It took most of my adult life for me to understand the thought on the opposite page. Results were what my whole existence was all about. Get the grades, win the game, get a better backhand, make more money, set sales records, lower my golf handicap, work faster, work smarter and on and on and on. Almost everything I did was a means to an end. Much of the time I wasn't enjoying the means.

See if the following scenario, or something similar, has ever happened in your life. I'm playing golf in a foursome on a beautiful day, and, sooner or later, maybe as early the first hole, somebody makes a mistake, like missing a chip shot and then three putts. The player is immediately upset. The next hole holds some more challenges for him, and he gets downright

~ ~

disgusted with himself, and communicates his peevishness to the rest of us.

I step outside of the situation and look around. It is a beautiful day. There is a gentle breeze. The sky is as blue as it gets, and the blossoms of spring are all over the place. And this guy not only doesn't appear to be aware of it. It seems as if he could care less.

It becomes obvious, this person isn't having any fun. His whole perspective is based on results. He wants par and he wants it now.

Many times in these situations I have been tempted to say, "Isn't it great that we have the chance to play golf together on such a super day?" But I didn't want to risk having a putter bent over my head.

I feel badly that some people's enjoyment of the game of golf, *or the game of life,* has to be so tied up in a score. But then I suspect that these people probably act the same way in business. Results, results, results. And not much fun.

Many years ago, when I was consumed with a major business venture, a new friend took the time to make an unusual wall hanging for me — a curved piece of wood with some dried wild flowers inserted in one end. With a wood burning tool she engraved these words:

Along the way,
Take time to smell the flowers.

~ ~ ~~ ~ ~~ ~ ~~ ~ ~~ ~ ~~ ~ ~~ ~ ~~ ~

That was 25 years ago, and I still have her gift. It took several of those years for me to fully appreciate the saying.

Today things are different. I will not let a day go by without being aware of the process of living and seeking some way to enjoy. No longer is the fun of a tennis match, or a golf game, ruined by a few missed shots or who won or lost.

Unlike many golfers, I love to practice. I call it my Zen time. I try to stay focused on the now, the present, being aware of my surroundings and enjoying the moment, the sky, the majesty of the mountains in the background, and the fun of trying to let the inner me hit the ball.

And then when I'm on the golf course I try to stay aware that it isn't making the putt or missing it that really counts. What counts is having the *opportunity* to putt. The joy of life is in being able to participate. That is when you are taking the time to smell the flowers.

The following thought from an unknown author is worth contemplating:

This moment — whatever it brings —
Is the gift.
Our celebration of today creates the laugh
lines on the face of tomorrow.

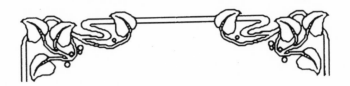

The unexamined life is not worth living.

— *Socrates 470-399 BC*

CHAPTER 9

Socrates was a wise man.

Understatement? Probably! His thoughts have been studied and discussed by scholars around the world. But I feel that a little more discussion, between you and me, wouldn't hurt anything — and might do some good.

Why did this great philosopher believe that an unexamined life is not worth living?

My interpretation of an unexamined life may not be what Socrates had in mind, but I take it to mean that you have lived your life without reflection on the past to make the present and the future better.

It seems that if one reason for our existence is to become the best we can become, then we must be more aware of who we are and

~ ~

what we can do in order to work toward that
purpose.

How can you become more aware? If you
will take the time to create an inventory of your
strengths and your weaknesses, your attitudes
and your talents, and then make a decision to
become stronger at what you're good at and less
weak at what you're not, you will be well on the
way. It is important that you commit these obser-
vations and decisions to paper since it is so easy
to forget your good intentions.

The easy part is to decide to change. The
hard part is to stay with your decision long
enough to make it happen. Changing requires
risk which calls for courage. But when you find
that courage — you will be fully participating in
life. And *that* will make your existence here
meaningful *and* purposeful.

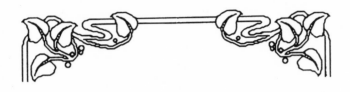

Over Fred Astaire's fireplace
in Beverly Hills was a yellowed
MGM interoffice memo,
a souvenir of the dancer's
first screen test.
Dated 1933 and sent
by the testing director
to his superior,
it reads:

"Fred Astaire.
Can't act.
Slightly bald.
Can dance a little."

CHAPTER 10

I wonder what went through the late Fred Astaire's mind when he heard the results of his first screen test? Was his confidence damaged, his Ego bruised? I wonder if he thought of throwing in the towel and finding a "real job?" I wonder if anyone else urged him to do just that?

Or do you suppose he believed so strongly in himself and his ability that there was no way to stop him? I guess you and I will never know, but whatever happened, how fortunate for the millions of people who enjoyed his acting and dancing.

Have you ever doubted yourself because of the negative opinion of someone else? If you're human, you have. Maybe more times than you like to think about.

~ ~

However, the moment you choose, like Fred Astaire, to ignore negative influences, to believe in yourself despite the people who would sway you from your purpose, you have the opportunity to make the most of your life. You may or may not have the talent to sing and dance your way into the hearts of millions, but you do have the talent to reach out and touch at least one other life, and in doing so experience part of the answer to the *big* question, "Why am I here?"

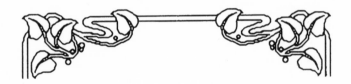

*True happiness is not made in
getting something.
True happiness is becoming
something.*

— *Elder Marvin J. Aston*

CHAPTER 11

For years, when I was riding the crest of material and financial success, I felt a disturbing sense of unease. I didn't know why. I had a wonderful wife, great children, close friends, nice cars, a beautiful home, and yet I was not at peace. I was blessed in many ways, yet something was missing.

I began to search for answers. I questioned my career in life insurance and asked myself what else I might do if money were not a factor. Would I want to be an Attorney? Accountant? Architect? Banker? Physician? Dentist? Corporate president? Scientist? None of these. I decided my job was not the problem. Then what was the source of my emptiness?

~ ~

It took more years on the treadmill, and a couple of major adversities, before I caught a glimpse of the source of my dissatisfaction.

Keeping busier and busier for the purpose of acquiring more and more was holding me captive in a vacuum of emptiness.

No great flash of light opened my eyes, but eventually I began to understand the answer isn't in the getting, it is in the becoming.

And then a friend shared these words with me:

"God doesn't care what you do. He only cares who you are."

What do these words mean? I think they mean that if you fail to develop who you are, the Spirit inside you that's yearning to grow, you may spend your life doing and acquiring, and never get as big as your soul can be.

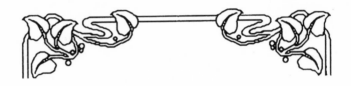

*Everybody has something
to overcome.
Mine is just more obvious.*

— John Rinehart

CHAPTER 12

Before I knew John Rinehart's story, I was struck by his friendly, outgoing spirit. Each time we saw each other he was in an up mood and seemed to have an almost childlike quality of confidence. I didn't know exactly what was wrong with his leg, or how he lost his arm, until I had the opportunity to sit in an audience and listen to him tell his story.

John was born without a right leg and sometime later the doctors were forced to amputate his right arm just below the elbow in order to save his life. Nevertheless, when he was just a boy, he learned to ride a bike with his leg fitted with a prosthesis. The prosthesis kept hindering him until finally he convinced his Dad he could learn to ride one-legged.

~ ~

I wonder when he first dreamed of winning the World Championship for Disabled Cyclists? Or at what moment he made an irrevocable promise to himself to do whatever it took to reach that dream?

As I listened to John's story I became aware of the mental and physical challenges he had to overcome, not the least of which was the negative input from others who felt he had no chance.

Yet, against all the odds, a two-year exhaustive training schedule culminated in France in 1989 when John captured the World Championship for Disabled Cyclists at age 24. He then went on to win three more world championships when he was 25, 26 and 29.

I watched a video of John in his racing gear going all out on his bike with his one leg. It was unbelievable. I felt privileged to know this young man who won against all the odds.

And then John said something so powerful that it has stayed with me ever since. He said, "Everyone has something to overcome. Mine is just more obvious."

Here was a young man who had gained a perspective that gave him wisdom beyond his years. He understood that we all have challenges. At one point in his life, a moment of truth, he had to make a decision. Either his

~ ~

disabilities could stand in his way, or he could rise above them and create the life he dreamed of.

Bruce Barton, an American author and businessman during the first part of this century, wrote an enduring thought that captures John's determination:

Nothing splendid has ever been achieved except by those who dared believe that something inside of them was superior to circumstance.

As you think about John and imagine what it took to reach the top, what it took to win four world championships, ask yourself this question: "What thoughts do I hold that are keeping me from becoming a world champion human being?" If you think about them long enough you'll realize that no matter what your answer is, your way to the top can be no more difficult than John Rinehart's. If he can overcome and conquer, *so can you!*

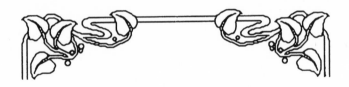

*One of Life's
Most Important Lessons:*

*Don't sweat the small stuff —
Everything is small stuff.*
                    — Author unknown

CHAPTER 13

Once, when I was newly married and without enough money to pay bills, I received a $35 ticket for rolling through a stop sign. This was more than 40 years ago, and $35 was a lot of money. In fact it was ten percent of my monthly wage.

I was devastated — sick to my stomach. How could I possibly find the money. This was not small stuff. This was *big* stuff. And I was sweating. Yet find the money we did, and we went on with our lives.

It was a long time, and many much more significant challenges later, before I had gained enough perspective to realize that events which appear to have negative impact at the moment may be blessings in disguise. Eventually I began to learn to accept and let go.

How about you? How many times in your life have you been involved in a situation that assumed gigantic proportions but you realized, in retrospect, it was really not life changing?

The fact is, if you place the negative things that happen to you in balance against the good things that happen to you — "Everything is small stuff." And, in the really big picture of life, all the day to day *stuff* can be pretty insignificant.

I think there also is another message here. It says:

Lighten up
Step outside yourself
Gain new perspectives
Take it in stride
Go with the flow

And realize that when you don't sweat the small stuff and make everything small stuff, life becomes a lot more fun.

Let me leave you with this little idea. If something happens to you which you can determine will not have a major negative impact on your life five years from now — then simply — *let it go!*

∞

~ ~

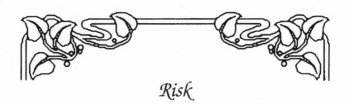

Risk

To laugh is to risk appearing the fool.
To weep is risk appearing sentimental.
To reach out to another is to risk involvement.
To expose feelings is to risk exposing your true self.
To place your ideas, your dreams before a crowd is to risk their loss.
To love is to risk not being loved in return.
To live is to risk dying. To hope is to risk despair.
To try is to risk failure.
But risks must be taken, because the greatest hazard in life is to risk nothing.
The person who risks nothing, does nothing, has nothing, is nothing.
He may avoid suffering and sorrow, but he cannot learn, feel, change, grow, love, live.
Only the person who risks is free.
— Author Unknown

CHAPTER 14

Why do people fear risk? I've discovered that most of us avoid risk not so much from the standpoint of threat to personal safety as from the threat of revealing ourselves and our ideas to the opinions of others.

In my long career in the life insurance business, I faced rejection daily, and in the early years was failing because I was trying to avoid it. My older and wiser friends kept telling me that it was not me people were rejecting, it was the idea of life insurance. It didn't feel that way to me.

Eventually I had to learn to place my determination to succeed above my fear of rejection. I had to make the necessary calls and adopt an attitude that those who rejected me/insurance would never get the chance to create a long term

~ ~

friendship with a nice guy. I was able to make this strategy work — most of the time.

In what part of your life are you hesitating to take risks. Relationships? Changing careers? Having a family? Risking looking like a klutz while you learn how to play golf? Why don't you give yourself a good look and see how much risk you are avoiding. Then determine how your life could be changed if you risked. Think about the following words by Guillaume Apollinaire:

> *"Come to the edge."*
> *"No, we will fall."*
> *"Come to the edge."*
> *"No, we will fall."*
> *"Come to the edge."*
> **He pushed them, and they flew.**

We all do less than we can, but — *there is no excuse for not trying to be more.*

My hope is that you will decide to go to the edge.

It's scary. But it's worth it. It's the stuff life is made of.

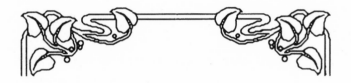

Love thy neighbor as thyself.
— *The Holy Bible*

CHAPTER 15

Never has a teaching been talked about more and followed less than this one. The Christian faith accepts this statement as one of the greatest commandments. Yet all religions seem to embrace it in some fashion or other. So why do we uniformly fail to practice it?

I think what has happened is that we follow the commandment according to the word rather than the intent. We love our neighbor just about as much as we love ourselves. And that isn't much.

Most of us have never come to accept ourselves for the beautiful Spirits we are, with the result that it is very difficult to see that Spirit in others. If we continually disparage ourselves, if we think of ourselves as being less than we should be, how can we transmit anything but

~ ~

those kind of thoughts to our neighbor? You can't give love if you don't own love.

Maybe if this commandment ordered us to "Love thyself unconditionally first, and then give that love away to thy neighbor," we'd be more willing to begin the process of learning to love ourselves.

I urge you to do everything in your power to start that process. If you've already begun maybe you can pick up the pace a bit. Start today. Let go of the past. Let go of the guilt you may have carried for years. Forgive yourself.

If you can peel back the layers of onion skin which are hiding your true Spirit, eventually you will like yourself, for the Spirit you are covering up is the expression of the light within. And when you can see that shining light in you, you will be able to see it in others. And "Love thy neighbor as thyself" will become who you are and what you do.

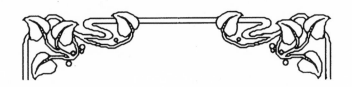

Life has its four seasons:
Fall, Winter, Spring and Summer.
You will have many Winters.
But remember,
As certain as it is that your life
will have its Winters,
You must always believe
That the Spring is sure to follow.
            — Author Unknown

CHAPTER 16

Each day offers the opportunity for you to experience any one of life's four seasons. Maybe it would be nice if it were Spring all the time with its fresh start and promise of a sunny future. But that is not the way life is.

Each person reacts differently to his or her own personal Winters. Some accept and go on. Some insist in wallowing in self pity, prolonging the rain and the snow. I have often observed two people facing exactly the same challenge with completely opposite perspectives.

About this negative and positive aspect of human nature, Abraham Lincoln said:

"The pessimist sees the difficulty in every opportunity. The optimist sees the opportunity in every difficulty."

~ ~

Several years ago a major university conducted a study on the effect of dysfunctional families on siblings. One case revolved around two brothers in their 30's who had been raised by an alcoholic father. One brother was very successful and had a good life. The other brother was foundering in the dregs of society. When each was asked by the researcher to what he attributed his way of life, both replied with exactly the same words, "What would you expect with a father like mine?"

In other words, it is how you *perceive* your circumstances that will eventually determine your real happiness in life.

The next time you find yourself in the middle of a bad, personal storm be aware of the *promise* of good things which can flow from this adversity. And as you hold on to this perspective an interesting phenomena is likely to occur — Spring may come early this year.

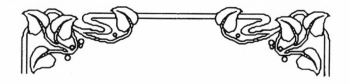

Aerodynamically,
it is impossible
for the bumble bee to fly.
But nobody told the bee.

— *Author Unknown*

CHAPTER 17

Here is this bumble bee flying from flower to flower, living out its purpose because it doesn't realize that science can prove its limitations. Wouldn't it be great if we humans were blessed with the bumble bee's ignorance? Imagine the life a person could design if limiting thinking was not a factor.

I recall a couple of statements made several years ago by scientists at the Brain Research Department at UCLA. One conclusion was that the potential of the human mind was *infinite*. The other was that humans, at this point in time, do not have the imagination to imagine their potential. I have thought about this last statement many times and wondered why it is we can't imagine our potential. I've decided it is because we are so busy imagining our limits that

~ ~

we don't leave time to imagine the possible. In other words, we fail to develop our potential because we use our imagination to put a lid on it.

Science tells us that our right brain is the primary source of our imagination. This is where our pictures are held. That is the good news. The bad news is that some sources say that possibly 75 percent of the pictures the average person holds in his right brain are of a negative nature.

In Marianne Williamson's *A Return To Love,* are these words addressing the human tendency to embrace the negative:

> *Our deepest fear is not that we are inadequate.*
> *Our deepest fear is that we are powerful beyond measure.*
> *It is our light, not our darkness, that most frightens us.*
> *We ask ourselves:*
> *"Who am I to be brilliant, gorgeous, talented and fabulous?"*
> *Actually, who are you not to be?*
> *You are a child of God.*
> *Your playing small doesn't serve the world.*
> *There is nothing enlightened about shrinking so that other people won't feel insecure around you.*

~ ~ ~~ ~ ~~ ~ ~~ ~ ~~ ~ ~~ ~ ~~~

We are all meant to shine, as children do.
We were born to make manifest the glory
of God that is within us.
It's not just in some of us, it is in
everyone.
And as we let our own light shine, we
unconsciously give other people the
permission to do the same.
As we're liberated from our own fear, our
presence automatically liberates
others.

The main source of the limits to who you could be and what you could do comes not from who you think you are, but rather from who you think you are not. As quoted above, "It is our light, not our darkness, that frightens us."

If, as the researchers at UCLA concluded, your potential truly is infinite, then it also *must* be unlimited for changing harmful, self-defeating perceptions — changing the 75 percent negative to 75 percent positive.

The next time you catch yourself imagining the negative, take time to recall Williamson's words. Then remember the bumble bee who doesn't know it can't fly.

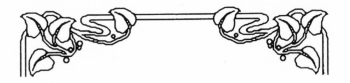

Pursue learning as if you were
going to live forever.
Live as if you were going
to die tomorrow.

— *Author unknown*

CHAPTER 18

Many people live their lives opposite to the words on the adjoining page. They act as if they were going to live forever, and fail to pursue learning because they think there is not enough time.

Why should you learn more? The best reason is because it is like treasure hunting. Only through learning and putting your acquired knowledge into action can you discover the treasure that is you. Only through searching can you make the difference you were put here to make. You have been given the gift of your mind. Make sure you say thank you by using it.

Living as if you were going to die tomorrow does not mean you should adopt a devil-may-care, drink-and-be-merry attitude. It does mean living in the present, to the very best

~ ~

of your ability. There is no second chance. Once the present becomes the past, it is written in stone. That is an absolute — at least on this plane.

How do you live in the present? You accept that there is only *now*. You replace anger and resentment with love and forgiveness — *now*. You spend time with those who count, doing things which count — *now*. You become more concerned with who you are than what you do. You appreciate the beauty in nature and the wonder of creation. You say "thank you." Again and again. Moment by moment. Now.

Reward yourself with some quiet time and ask these questions: Today have I studied new ways to make life better for myself and those around me? Did I live today as I would want my final day to be lived? If you can answer "yes," to such questions, even now and then, you are one of the lucky ones.

~ ~ ~~ ~ ~~ ~ ~~ ~ ~~ ~ ~~ ~ ~~ ~ ~~~

Don't Quit

When things go wrong as they sometimes will,
When the road you're trudging seems all uphill,
When the funds are low, and the debts are high;
And you want to smile, but have to sigh;
When care is pressing you down a bit—
Rest if you must, but don't you quit.
Success is failure turned inside out;
The silver tint of the clouds of doubt;
And you can never tell how close you are;
It may be near when it seems afar.
So stick to the fight when you're hardest hit.
It's when things go wrong that you mustn't quit.

— Author Unknown

CHAPTER 19

Sometimes the struggle gets over-whelming. You feel like looking up to the heavens and saying, "Why me, God?" It just doesn't seem fair. It happens to everyone. Some handle it and some don't. It's the ones who don't that I feel sad for. They lose their perspective and are in danger of never getting it back. They may fall into the role of permanent victim. And it doesn't have to be.

In spite of some significant adversities I've had in my life, I was blessed with an attitude that urged me to look around and notice someone who had it worse. This outlook allowed me to put things into proper perspective.

Many years ago it was necessary to take our firstborn, Gary, to a children's hospital in the big city. While there I observed children in

~ ~

various stages of personal suffering beyond anything I had ever seen. There were children who were destined to live an entire lifetime with a crippling disease. There were children who, like our own son, would not live out the year. My own suffering paled compared to theirs. The impact of that visit never left me.

In the years that followed, when things were not going my way, I found myself thinking about those children, and I was able to accept my problems, and count my blessings.

The next time you're in the dumps and the burden seems too great, why not visit the children in a hospital and see if you don't gain a new look at what is going on in your life.

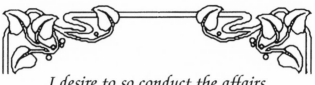

I desire to so conduct the affairs
of this administration
that if, at the end,
when I come to lay down
the reins of power,
I have lost every other friend
on earth,
I shall at least have one friend left,
and that friend shall be deep down
inside of me —
I am not bound to win,
but I am bound to be true.
I am not bound to succeed,
but I am bound to
live up to the light I have.

Abraham Lincoln

(Shortly after his narrow victory over McClellan when it seemed that the whole nation — North and South — was against him.)

CHAPTER 20

Can you imagine what this world would be like if every child brought into being could live the thought expressed by President Lincoln? What a society this would be.

Lincoln's words were a code of honor for him and in them you might find the inspiration to fashion your own Affirmation of Excellence.

Your Affirmation can be a promise to yourself that regardless of circumstances you will act according to your personally-defined values, and regardless of the opinions of others continue to feel good about yourself.

You need to put your Affirmation of Excellence into words. You're probably not going to become all that you can become unless you define yourself on paper. You will need reminding of exactly what it is you want your

~ ~

life to stand for. And you will be tempted by yourself and others to stray from the principles you've articulated in your Affirmation. But if you remain firm you will win, and live the life of freedom. The only people who are truly free in this world are the ones who decide what is important and conduct their lives accordingly.

If you decide to design an Affirmation of Excellence, I don't think Abraham Lincoln would mind if you included his words:

> *I am not bound to win,*
> *but I am bound to be true.*
> *I am not bound to succeed,*
> *but I am bound to live up*
> *to the light I have.*

~ ~

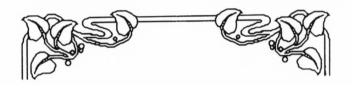

When your past
controls your present,
your future becomes
what you were
instead of what you could be.

— *Bill O'Hearn*

CHAPTER 21

The trouble with living the present based upon what happened in the past is that you don't have the whole picture. Oh, you have a picture of what happened and what you can do. You just don't have a picture of what is possible.

Steven Covey observed that everything is created twice, once in the imagination, once in reality. If this is so, then it seems to me that if you expect to create a more fulfilling life for yourself, you are going to have to use your imagination more.

The problem is that you are already using part of your brain to hold the pictures of the past. And those pictures are so powerful that they can control all your actions if you allow them to do so.

~ ~ ~~ ~ ~~ ~ ~~ ~ ~~ ~ ~~ ~ ~~ ~ ~~ ~

How do you go about creating new pictures? It's easy to say, "Just do it." But that is too tough for most of us. The easier way is to daydream, to *imagine* what is possible and then to *write down* how you would like your life to be. Once you have your dream on paper, the next phase can begin.

In your imagination create a vivid picture of the new you and your new life. It is important to actually feel the pictures you are seeing. If you can see the new you and *feel* the new you, pretty soon you will *be* the new you.

Remember, your dream, and your imagining of what the future can be, must be continually upgraded because any change that does occur in the present will inevitably become part of the past.

But that is what makes life challenging and fun. There will *always* be new horizons to conquer and new mountains to climb.

~ ~

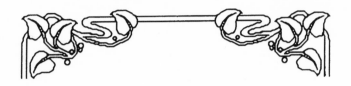

*You've had your successes,
and you've had your failures.
If you are somewhere in the grasp of
the latter,
remember —
Beneath the ashes the ember still
glows.*

— *Bill O'Hearn*

Chapter 22

When you tried the very best you knew how. When you've paid the price and experienced the pain of going the extra mile. When you've given everything and then some. When you know you can make it in spite of negative circumstances and cynical critics, but, when all is said and done, you failed — that is life at its toughest.

Failure puts a negative spin on things. Call it bleak. Or gray. Or ugly. Your energy is spent. Your mind is crying. Your confidence is shattered. And you just don't give a rip anymore.

Sound familiar? If not, it will — sooner or later. It's part of the journey. Not the best part by far, but definitely a part. And when it happens to you, whether it is in a relationship, or a business venture or whatever, one thing is certain —

~ ~

sooner or later you are going to have to pull yourself up and get on with your life.

How do you do that? Especially when you're not even sure you want to do anything. Let me give you a couple of thoughts.

First, you must find a way to step outside of yourself. To become an observer of you and your situation. You'll probably have to create some quiet time in order to do this. Then you have to ask some important questions. Such as: "Do I have *anything* to be thankful for?" The temptation will be to say, "Hell no!" But if you really look, you'll discover something to be thankful for. How about good health, or a playful child, or living in a country offering future opportunities or even the chance to watch a beautiful sunset? Or how about the fact that you are alive and able to recover? It surely must be better than the alternative.

Eventually you'll be ready for the big question:

"Does my failure serve a bigger purpose than appears on the surface?"

There always seems to be a bigger purpose. It may take you a while to discover what it is, but if you refuse to give in you will find it.

~ ~

One purpose that will appear is in the form of an opportunity to go to the next level in your growth as a human being.

Remember, deep down inside you is a glowing ember that is your real core, your unde-featable Spirit. Failure offers the chance to fan that ember and discover the bigger dimension of you. When you realize how much power that creates, you will go on with renewed vitality and confidence — and you will have discovered this simple truth:

"Because I lost, I have gained."

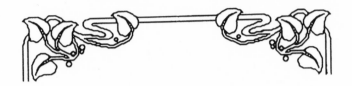

Be careful of what
you go after
in life,
You may end up
with your pocket full
and your mind empty.

— *Author unknown*

CHAPTER 23

Too many people are spending too much time heading toward too little.

Too little of what life is all about. I know. I've been there and done that: "Earn more money. Get a bigger house. Drive a better car. Accumulate wealth so that someday we can be secure, relaxed and live a little."

I don't think the words on the opposite page refer to the fact that we should be accumulating knowledge instead of money. I think they mean something deeper than that. So let me change just one word in the quotation.

Be careful of what you go after in life,
You may end up with your pocket full
And your Spirit empty.

~ ~ ~ ~ ~ ~ ~ ~ ~ ~ ~ ~ ~ ~ ~ ~ ~ ~ ~ ~

Today's frantic pace can push us into that undesirable position. There is no time to slow down and nourish the Spirit. We use money as a hallmark of success, and we go after more and more of it just to prove we are okay. And in the getting we forget that we are okay to begin with, and that no amount of money will make us any better.

In the pursuit of things we sometimes forget to take time to quiet the mind. To acknowledge our Source and our destination. To contemplate what we could accomplish for ourselves and others if we but tried.

Why not give some extra thought to the direction you are heading. Just to make sure it is the path you want.

Let me leave you with these words written by Margaret Fuller, an American critic and reformer who lived from 1810 to 1850:

> **Men for the sake of making a living forget to live.**

Man or woman — don't let that happen to you.

~ ~

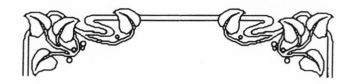

God grant me the serenity to accept
the things I cannot change,
The courage to change
the things I can,
And the wisdom to know
the difference.
　　　　　　　　　— *Reinhold Niebuhr*

CHAPTER 24

The prayer by Reinhold Niebuhr has been used by Alcoholics Anonymous for many years. I don't know when I first heard it, but I have since come to feel that it could be a standard of performance for everyone.

Over the past several years, as I thought about how I might apply this inspiring prayer in my own life, I began to see a pattern of human behavior that often appeared to follow the saying, but in fact fell far short.

Let me see if I can explain. I believe the substance of Niebuhr's thought lies in the words: *And the wisdom to know the difference.*

Too many times I have accepted a situation I assumed I could not change, and failed to give myself the opportunity to make something better. And much too often I have seen people

~ ~ ~ ~ ~ ~ ~ ~ ~ ~ ~ ~ ~ ~ ~ ~ ~ ~ ~ ~

stuck in unfavorable situations because they lacked the insight to know what they could change and what they couldn't.

Has this ever happened to you? Let me urge you not to accept any circumstances unless you are absolutely certain, *beyond all doubt,* that they cannot be changed.

And when, with courage, you have forced your heart and mind to try over and over again, win or lose, you will find that you have developed a greater wisdom to know the difference. In the struggle your life will take on meaning far beyond anything you can imagine. And therein lies the fun of the game of life.

~ ~

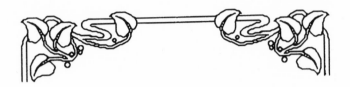

The real measure of a full life
Lies not in its achievements
or in its length,
But rather
In the amount of love
That is given and received.

— *Bill O'Hearn*

CHAPTER 25

$\mathbf{B}$eing a person who has spent most of his life concerned with achievements and in personal longevity, I sometimes wonder how I evolved enough to think the thought expressed on the opposite page. If I had to give you a straight answer to my own question, I would have to tell the story of the famous judge who was being interviewed by the press. When asked to explain to what he attributed his success, he answered, "Good judgement." When the interviewer persisted and asked how he obtained his good judgement he replied, "Experience!" When the interviewer then asked how the famous judge got experience, he replied, "Bad judgement." Much of where I am today comes from the same sequence.

~ ~

I now feel that achievements and things are part of life's experiences but the measure of where real joy comes from revolves around love given and love received. Why not take a moment and reflect on when you experienced that really alive feeling — when you experienced *real* joy. I doubt that you will say on your deathbed that the only real joy you found in life was at the office and that you wished you had spent more time there. And you probably didn't find it when you bought a new car, although I must admit that does have a pretty good feel to it. More likely you experienced real joy when you saw the light in a child's eyes as you helped her discover a new wonder. Or helped someone less fortunate. Or gave of yourself to a friend. Or simply offered and accepted love with no strings attached.

So if you want to experience life at its best, seek out ways to give love. Three things will happen. You'll discover love coming back. Your life will have full measure. And the world will be better because you were here.

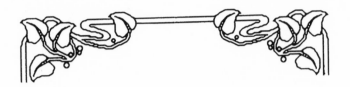

The great and glorious masterpiece
of man
is how to live with purpose.
— Michel de Montaigne

CHAPTER 26

I can't speak for anyone but myself, but I'll tell you right up front that my biggest challenge for much of my adult life has been to identify *my* purpose. Why am I here? What am I supposed to accomplish? How do I touch the brush to the canvas of *my* masterpiece? What is holding me back?

I know that there are those out there who do not even suspect that having a purpose is important. They are having enough trouble just surviving. I believe, though, that deep down inside of every human being is an inner desire to count for something — to make the world a better place for having lived. Most of us just get that desire buried early on. The good news is that it is still there, and can be uncovered. So why aren't we making it happen?

~ ~ ~~ ~ ~ ~~ ~ ~~ ~ ~~ ~ ~~ ~ ~~ ~ ~~~

You know what I think it is? I think that we are too caught up in the rush of *doing*. We are too *busy* to seek our purpose.

Isn't this a strange paradox? We are put here for a purpose, yet there is no time to seek it. Bummer.

My personal philosophy is that we are put here to serve, to grow and to learn to love. But too many times in my life I got so caught up in the chaos of daily scurrying that I lost sight of this belief. I ignored that small, inner voice which urged me to slow down and be on purpose.

I received a phone call one night from a young woman I had watched grow from infancy to adulthood. She wanted to thank me for having been a positive influence in her life. She mentioned words like skiing, tennis, singing, ukulele. She never once mentioned what I spent the majority of my time doing those years, which was selling life insurance. I was never aware that I was having a positive impact on her. Isn't it interesting that it all happened while I was having fun and just being me? Maybe *that* was when I was touching the brush to the canvas.

I believe each one of us has been given marvelous powers to be more than we are. Discovering those powers and unveiling the

~ ~

masterpiece which lies within *you* is what the journey is all about. Your life is like an artist's canvas, and it's *your* choice as to what you create. But whatever you choose — make it fun. And — make it you!

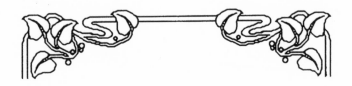

Ideas without action
are like waves
crashing on the shore,
for a moment
full of energy,
suddenly no more.

— *Todd Yorke*

CHAPTER 27

Many times I have watched people become excited about a great idea. It seemed to permeate their whole being. They literally became different persons as they thought about what they were going to do. They had a vision. They could clearly see the end result. They had purpose and, at the moment, commitment. Yet it all came to naught.

What happens between the conception of a good idea, yours or mine, and its fruition? Well, I can't speak for you but in my case I know exactly what happens. My "idea of the moment" dies because it requires more than excitement and thinking. Sooner or later it requires *action* and *commitment — on a continuing basis*. A dedication to results, no matter what the price.

~ ~

I have seen people excited about the possibility of becoming accomplished with a musical instrument. They were full of energy and determination. They signed up for lessons, put themselves on a highly disciplined practice schedule and started their vision. Soon, however, practice became burdensome. All work and no play. Eventually the instrument began to accumulate dust, as did the dream.

Why did this happen? Maybe it was because the dream lacked passion, or the end result became too vague, or the price seemed too high. But, when you are willing to pay the price to bring an idea into being, the price — I've learned — is hardly ever as big as you imagine. It is worth the struggle to keep your idea alive.

The next time you get an idea that brings light to your eyes, reach deep down inside of yourself and make a commitment to the end result — regardless of the *perceived* sacrifice. You'll like the feeling, the sense of purpose, and eventually, the pride of accomplishment. But, most importantly, you'll feel good about you.

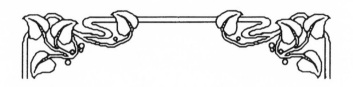

Doubt sees the obstacles,
Faith sees the way.
Doubt sees the darkest night,
Faith sees the day.
Doubt dreads to take a step,
While faith soars on high.
Doubt questions, "Who believes?"
Faith answers, "I."

— Author unknown

CHAPTER 28

Many times I have silently given great lip service to my ability and talent, but often at the moment of truth I have backed away from "Going for the Gold" — refusing by default to stretch myself toward my possibilities because deep inside I felt I was not good enough.

A good example might be my first book, *From the Heart of a Child,* which I put off for several years partly because I was defeated before I even began by nagging doubts.

It was my *Ego* filling me with doubt. Ego, that part of my inner being that doesn't like risk for fear of looking the fool. Ego, with its strong inner voice argued for me to stay in my limiting comfort zone, shrink away from taking chances, make fear of failure the overriding emotion. Ego is a killer of human potential.

~ ~

Intellectually it was easy for me to convince myself I could be a hero. Emotionally, it was easier to be a coward. Have you ever been there?

What can you do when Spirit beckons and Ego argues? You must go outside of yourself. You must rise above your everyday thinking, elevate yourself so that you can understand there is far more to you and this world than protective Ego. You must believe there are *infinite* possibilities for you. How do you do that? Faith! Faith that you were put here for a higher purpose than you may be able to see. Faith that when the student is ready, the teacher will appear. Faith that no effort goes unrewarded. Faith that you *can* and *will* make a difference.

When Doubt, fueled by Ego, rears its ugly head, remember, you were born to win. You and your Spirit can make dreams come true — and with Faith, that is all you need.

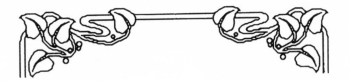

Then is Then
Now is Now

 — *Dr. Ed Timmons*

CHAPTER 29

I don't want to sound overly dramatic, but the phrase on the opposite page saved my life.

It was in 1977, and Dr. Ed Timmons, from Louisiana State University, was in Oregon giving a three-day seminar to a group men in the life insurance industry. Much good came out of that seminar, but the greatest good for me were these words:

Then is Then and Now is Now.

When I say this phrase saved my life. I mean my psychological life, not my physical life, although who knows, doesn't the first have an impact on the second?

I was educated in the primary grades at a Catholic school. Part of my religious training

~ ~

involved a course in *Guilt.* I don't know if that was the intention, but it certainly was the effect. Imagine, 12 years old and destined for Hell! You would enjoy a good laugh at my interpretation of Sin.

And I carried that guilt until I met Dr. Timmons.

In three short days he blessed me with a new perspective about the past and I, for whatever reason, was able to let it all go. I decided that any more time spent in the guilt-ridden past was detrimental to a guilt-free present.

Are you carrying around a burden of guilt? You can let it go, you know. Easier than you think. You do have to accept that what is done is done and cannot be undone. If there are amends to make — make them. But remember — *the past is gone.* All you have is this very moment. It's yours to do with as you like. And I can personally guarantee you that letting loose of guilt is a *really* good deal.

~ ~

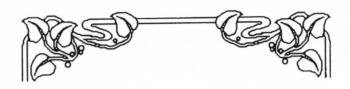

"Your task — to build a better
world," God said.
I answered, "How? — the world is
such a large place.
So complicated now — and I so
small and useless am.
There's nothing I can do."
But God, in all his wisdom, said,
"Just build a better you."

— *Author unknown*

CHAPTER 30

I wonder if any human being can comprehend the lasting effect of one person's decision to "build a better you." The lives touched by such a decision are legend. How many lives is imponderable. Yet so often we get caught up thinking that we can't even make a small contribution to the Big Picture.

Let's look at the consequences of a father's decision to be more patient with his daughter after hurting her feelings.

To develop more patience, the father must raise his expectations of himself. He will no longer accept impatience in himself. Next, he must create a vision of himself as a loving, caring and patient person. Then he can go back, in his imagination, and replay the unhappy event with his daughter, replacing his old self with a

~ ~

father who listened to his child with under-
standing. He can coach himself toward his new
goal with the words, "I am a wonderfully patient
man and really love showing this side of me to
my daughter." When he acts out his new vision
of himself long enough, he will begin to become
that person.

When this daddy starts showing more
patience in real life — *He is showing more love.*
How do you think his daughter will respond to
more love? Will she think better of herself?
When she thinks better of herself will that show
in her relationship with others? Will it show in
her performance at school? Will she have a
positive influence on her friends? Yes, to all of
these things. Her father's action will affect her
life forever and in turn affect the lives of those
she touches.

The effect of the positive waves that
emanate from that father's decision have the
potential to touch thousands of people. The good
will not stop even when the daughter departs this
world. The good goes on *forever.*

What if you make an irrevocable decision
to "build a better you"? And you make a
commitment to do this *each and every day for
the rest of your life?* Will your decision have an
impact on a few people, a thousand people, the

~ ~

whole world? Who knows how far you can reach?

Ask yourself this: "Would I like to make a difference in this world and be a star in the eyes of God?" This is how you do that:

Just Build a Better You.

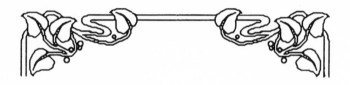

If the doors of perceptions
were cleansed,
everything would appear to man
as it is——-
infinite.

Wm. Blake 1796

CHAPTER 31

What powerful possibilities the words of William Blake offer us. They remind us that a cloak of limitation called perception, lies over each one of us.

It is difficult for humans to develop perspectives which conflict with their beliefs, but I would like you to consider what might be possible in your life if you perceived things differently.

I remember the perceptions I held as a teenager, and how much different they were from those I held as a 30-year-old. At each age my perceptions were *real*. Time and experience taught me new *perceived* realities.

So today as I look at Blake's words, written 200 years ago, I wonder why we haven't advanced very far into what might really be

~ ~

possible for us. Why haven't we been able to take the veil off our perceptions?

Of course, one look at the technological advancements of the past 50 years makes it appear that we have come a long way. Yet so much more is possible.

What about miracles? Most people wonder about miracles and relegate them to the supernatural. The human tendency is to stay rooted in what has been instead of imagining what could be. Yet I feel there is the possibility for miracles in all areas of life. They are waiting for us to believe enough to make them happen.

Think about these words of Edgar Mitchell, Apollo 14 astronaut:

> *There are no unnatural*
> *or supernatural phenomena,*
> *only very large gaps in our knowledge*
> *of what is natural.*
> *We should strive to fill*
> *those gaps of ignorance.*

If you can accept this thought then maybe that is the first step toward making miracles of your own. Miracle making begins by opening your mind to possibilities that heretofore did not exist in your thinking. Start by looking at what is going on in your life and allowing your intuition,

~ ~

instead of your logical mind, to guide you toward your highest possibilities.

Jules Verne, a writer of enormous imagination, added his vote to human potential when he wrote:

> ***What man can conceive,***
> ***Man can achieve.***

Why not take just a moment and listen to the Universe. Maybe there is a miracle waiting to take place in *your* life.

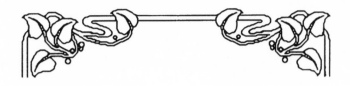

Ask and you will receive;
Seek and you will find;
Knock and it will be opened to you.
— *Matthew 7:7*

CHAPTER 32

Pretend with me that you are traveling in a far off land and you meet a stranger who offers to share a special parchment with you. He promises that it contains the answers to the life you have been seeking. You may feel unsure of his intentions, but you decide to investigate. After all, what can you lose?

When you unfold the parchment, these are the words inscribed on its surface:

Secrets For Becoming All You Can Become:

- *Realize the only limits are the ones you impose.*
- *When they say it can't be done — smile and do it anyway.*

~ ~

- *Remember that the Golden Rule is real — practice it!*
- *Your reality is only real to you. If there is part of it you don't like — change it.*
- *You were born with a purpose. Find it and follow it.*
- *Whatever you dream you can do — you can do!*
- *When troubled by circumstances, remember — Circumstances don't count.*
- *You were created to be a channel for love.*
- *Only when you give it away can you hope to get it back.*
- *Peace and Joy are found in the heart—not in things.*
- *Include your Guardian Angel when you talk to yourself.*
- *Listen to your imagination — it is the fountain of creation.*
- *Each day make the effort to grow, to serve and to love.*
- *To become all that you can become, you must first let go of who you are.*

A bit disappointed after reading the parchment, you look up at the stranger but he is

~ ~

already leaving. You call after him, "But where is the secret of life?" With a smile, as he waves goodbye, he says, "You have it in your hands *if only you will believe."*

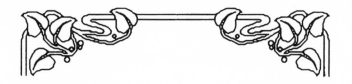

The Heart of the
Matter
is
Love

CHAPTER 33

When all the words are said, when all the thoughts are thought, it all comes down to one simple truth: the meaning of our human existence is based on love. And the heart of all that is or ever will be is defined by the action of love.

Love of others. Love of nature and all its creatures. Love of self. Love of your Source, and love of the opportunity to participate in this great earth adventure.

As you proceed on your journey, pause every once in awhile and take a love-check. Make sure you are treating yourself with the respect and caring which is your due. Then make sure that your light radiates out to touch others.

If at the end of the journey you can say that of all the things you have accomplished, the greatest was that you learned to love and then to give that love away, the world will be better for your having passed this way, and your purpose here will have been served.

Bill O'Hearn is a member of the National Speakers Association and is available for:

- Speeches
- Keynotes
- Workshops
- Seminars

To schedule him for your organization's most important event(s), please call:

503-694-2255
or
800-537-9991

To Order Bill O'Hearn's *Books*

	Price	Qty	Total
The Heart Of The Matter	12.95	_____	_____
From The Heart Of A Lion	11.95	_____	_____
From The Heart Of A Child	11.95	_____	_____
Shipping/Handling (1-2 books)	2.50	_____	_____
Each additional book	1.00	_____	_____
Total Order		_____	_____

Name: _____

Address: _____

City/State/Zip: _____

Phone; Bus.: _____ Home: _____

If paying with credit card, please complete
information below:
[ ] Visa   [ ] MasterCard

_____ _____ _____
   Card #   Expiration Date   Your Signature

Please note, on the back of this form, to whom
you would like the inscription made out.

Please return this order form with check or
money order payable to:

Entheos Publishing Company
P.O. Box 970
Wilsonville, Oregon 97070

To Order Today Call
503-694-5800 or 800-537-9991
Or Fax: 503-694-2677